Planting For Colour Through The Year

Jackie Matthews

HH
HERMES
HOUSE

The edition published by Hermes House

© Anness Publishing Limited 2002 updated 2003..

Hermes House is an imprint of Anness Publishing Limited,
Hermes House, 88–89 Blackfriars Road, London SE1 8HA

Publisher: Joanna Lorenz
Production Controller: Joanna King

Publisher's Note:
The Reader should not regard the recommendations, ideas and techniques
expressed and described in this book as substitutes for the advice of a
qualified medical practitioner or other qualified professional.
Any use to which the recommendations, ideas and techniques
are put is at the reader's sole discretion and risk.

Printed in Hong Kong/China

3 5 7 9 10 8 6 4

CONTENTS

Introduction

We expect to find colour in our gardens, but to create stunning effects and ensure a continuous show throughout the year will require some understanding of how colour behaves and when plants are at their best. With planning, even the smallest gardens can provide year-round colour.

Year-round Colour

As the year progresses, different types of plant come into their own. Using the right mix of plants and blends of colour will ensure that a garden has plenty of colour the year round. In mixed borders, shrubs provide the basis of any planting, giving it structure as well as colour. These can be in-filled with a multitude of other types of plants, mostly herbaceous perennials, bulbs, and annuals, their seasonal time and

Above: *Yellows and creams blend to create a restful feel to this summer border.*

colour chosen to complement the more permanent plants. Beds devoted to particular types of plants can be planted up on a rotation basis.

Borders

Spring-flowering bulbs can be planted in borders used for summer bedding, providing colour early in the year. Herbaceous and mixed borders also benefit from a generous scattering of bulbs to help provide colour and interest until the late spring, when the early summer plants take over.

Left: *Irises and primulas dominate this late-spring border for a striking effect.*

Certainly, the flowers of some bulbs are short-lived compared with summer flowers (often no more than a couple of weeks at their peak), but this shortcoming is easily rectified by interplanting with spring bedding plants such as winter-flowering pansies, forget-me-nots and polyanthus. They ensure a superb display for more than a month, by which time the beds will probably have to be cleared when the ground is prepared for summer flowers. They also help to fill in around the base of tall bulbs such as tulips that can otherwise look rather stalky.

Make sure that mixed borders include shrubs that flower at different times of the year.

The planting schemes used by your local parks department can provide some useful ideas for successful colours and plants, especially if your plant knowledge is limited.

Above: The colourful bark of Salix *is at its best in the winter months.*

CONTAINERS

An ideal way to ensure a display of plants at their peak is to plant them in containers. This allows plants to be moved about as they come into flower and fade. Tubs, troughs, window boxes, and even hanging baskets can all be replanted for spring colour.

PERMANENT COLOUR

Annuals and perennials are wonderful for providing successional colour, but growing them does involve work – sowing, potting on, planting out, deadheading, dividing and clearing away dead matter. So some gardeners prefer to create most of their colour using more permanent plants such as heathers and evergreen shrubs, including conifers and ivies which require less maintenance.

Left: Dahlias provide strong colours for the autumn border.

Introduction

THE EFFECTS OF COLOUR

Colour has a strong influence on mood and you can use it in your garden to create different effects. Reds are restless and passionate, blues can be calming, yellows are cheerful. Colours also affect the tones of other colours next to them, creating slight changes in their appearance. The way colours work is explored in more detail later in the book.

Nothing in a garden is static and whatever effect you create will undergo changes through the day and according to the season. The colour of a flower or leaf will change as it develops, from bud to fall.

LIGHT

Each season has a different type of light, and this affects the hues of plants. Light also changes throughout the

Above: The copper-tinted leaves of the Phormium *make an interesting contrast with small, vivid geranium flowers.*

day. Pale flowers stand out in shade and at dusk, while bright ones seem to bleach out in the midday sun.

USING FOLIAGE

Most foliage is green, but the number of different greens is almost infinite. Careful arrangement of these various greens will enhance the display, but even more can be achieved by incorporating into the garden the large number of plants, especially shrubs, that have foliage in other colours, including yellow, gold, silver, white, purple and blue.

To enjoy coloured foliage at its best, remember that purple and silver-leaved plants need the sun to retain their colour; golden and yellow foliage, however, often need a dappled shade

Left: The various smoke bushes (Cotinus) *all have excellent purple foliage. They look especially effective when they are planted so that the evening sun shines through the leaves.*

Above: The variegated Hosta 'Golden Tiara', *with its creamy-edged leaves, brightens a shaded corner.*

as too much sun can scorch the leaves and too much shade causes them to turn greener.

VARIEGATED FOLIAGE

Some plants have leaves in two or more colours, known as "variegated" foliage. There are many different types of variegation. In shrubs most variations are gold, followed closely by cream and white. These have the effect of lightening any group of plants they are near. Green-on-green variegations also have a lightening effect, but variegations involving purples often introduce a more sombre mood.

Variegated plants should be used with discretion. They can become too "busy", and if several are planted together they tend to clash. Reserve them for use as accent plants, to draw the eye. They are useful in shade or in

Right: The purple foliage of Canna 'Roi Humber' *is eyecatching against red, yellow and green.*

a dark corner because they shine out and create interest in an otherwise unpromising or dull situation.

Although many variegated shrubs will tolerate full sun, many prefer a light, dappled shade, out of hot sun.

HOW TO USE THIS BOOK

Begin by reading *Choosing a Colour Scheme* which explains how colours work together. It is possible to install permanent colour in the garden, which remains constant through the changing seasons. The section entitled *Year-round Plants* describes the plants to use for this effect.

The following sections are each devoted to a season of the year. They explore successful seasonal colour combinations and catalogue the main jobs that need to be done in the garden.

Finally the *Seasonal Plant Chart* and a list of common names will help you with your planning.

Choosing a Colour Scheme

PLANTS ARE AVAILABLE IN A WONDERFUL RANGE OF COLOURS, WHICH
GIVES GARDENERS TREMENDOUS SCOPE WHEN DESIGNING AN AREA.
START BY PLANNING YOUR COLOUR SCHEME ON GRAPH PAPER USING
COLOURED PENCILS, TO GIVE YOU A BETTER IDEA OF THE END RESULT.

USING COLOUR

There is such vast choice of colour in
plants, that with a little imagination it
is possible to paint any picture you
like and create any mood you desire.

Not all colours mix well, so rather
than randomly scattering colours, it is
better to use them in drifts, placing
plants so that each has a harmonious
relationship with its neighbour. When
this is done, the eye can move effort-
lessly along a border, enjoying inher-
ent subtleties as it passes over a
thoughtfully blended whole.

If in doubt about colour combinations, bear in mind that white or blue
will go with almost any other colour,
and look good. Pastel shades are for-
giving colours. The ones to be careful
with are brilliant orange and strong
magenta, which could look discon-
certing when placed together.

BLENDING COLOURS

Unless you want a monochromatic
scheme, the basic principle is to blend
colours. If you want to use two different colours that oppose each other on
the colour wheel in close proximity,
you can sometimes find another
colour that will link them. Blue and
red are in stark contrast to each other,
and you may prefer to keep them apart
by placing a purple plant between
them, which will greatly improve the
appearance of the flower border.
Incorporating areas of interesting
foliage in suitable colours is often an
excellent way of linking and separating
blocks of colour.

*Left: Silver leaves, a dusty pink and the
crimson flowers of* Digitalis *are unified
by the purple* Aquilegia *and* Ajuga *which
both stimulate and please the eye.*

Above: The hot yellow and reds of the primulas contrast perfectly with the blue Myosotis.

LEAF COLOUR

Foliage plays an important part in any colour scheme and wonderful effects can be created by placing a stunningly different coloured flower against an interesting leaf colour. For instance the delicate pink of an opium poppy *(Papaver somniferum)* is beautifully set off against silver-grey leaves.

HOT AND COOL COLOURS

When you are decorating the whole mood of a room can change depending on whether you are using hot or cool colours. It is exactly the same when you are designing and planning a garden.

Hot colours – the flame reds and oranges – are lively and will bring a dash of excitement to a border. Intense blues will definitely cool things down,

and white imparts a general sense of purity and tranquillity. Each colour has many tones and shades and all of these can be found in flowers and the many varieties of foliage.

Pastel colours have a romantic quality, and are often suitable for a dull, grey climate. However, a garden devoted entirely to pale colours such as these can be rather boring.

THE COLOUR WHEEL

Artists and designers use what is known as a colour wheel, in which colours that are situated next to each other on the wheel have a sympathetic bond and will work well together. Purple and blue as well as blue and green, for example, look good together. Colours on opposite sides of the wheel are contrasting and may clash with each other. Orange, for instance, will stand out quite starkly against blue.

There are occasions, however, when combining opposing colours can be used to create a focal point or to add life in an otherwise bland scheme.

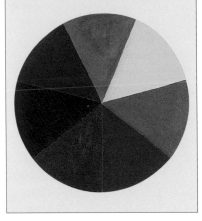

Colour in the Garden

As you plan for colour in the garden, decide which effect you wish to achieve. You can use calming, soft colours or include a bright, vibrant focal point or a hot border. You may even choose to create peace and tranquillity with a completely white border.

Using Hot Colours

Confine hot colours to one border, possibly as a centrepiece, but use softer colours in the other beds to ring in

Above: Kniphofias have several alternative names, of which "red-hot poker" aptly describes the colour of many of them. These shafts of hot colours are useful not only for their brightness, but also for their shape.

the changes and to provide a more tranquil planting area. It is possible to create a border containing nothing but red flowers, but it is always more interesting to have one that incorporates other hot colours as well. However, many people prefer to use a limited number of hot-coloured perennials in a cooler-coloured border, where they will act as a strong focal

point and make a dramatic statement. Red or yellow flowers are the strongest colours for impact.

Hot colours have a tendency to "advance" – that is, they seem much closer than they really are – so if you want to make a long border appear shorter than it is, plant the hot colours at the far end.

Use the different hues of foliage to link the hot colours with cool colours in the border.

Above: The glorious ruby-red flowers of Rhododendron 'Dopey'.

Using Cool Colours

Although blues are, in theory, cool colours, those blues that are tinged with red are warm. Combined with the warm pinks, the overall effect is

Above: The cool colours of Nemophilia menziesii *(Californian bluebell).*

one of cool calm. Use blues, purples and pinks, including many of the pastel shades, to achieve this effect.

Pastel colours create a misty effect, which means that they can be mixed together or dotted around. An even better effect can be achieved by using drifts of colour, merging the drifts.

Above: Use bright-red plants, such as Dahlia *'Bishop of Llandaff', as a bold focal point.*

RED FLOWERS

Amaranthus caudatus
Antirrhinum 'Scarlet Giant'
Begonia semperflorens 'Volcano'
Canna
Cleome hassleriana 'Cherry Queen'
Crocosmia 'Lucifer'
Dahlia
Geum "Mrs. J. Bradshaw'
Impatiens (various varieties)
Kniphofia (red hot poker)
Lobelia erinus 'Red Cascade'
Monarda 'Cambridge Scarlet'
Paeonia
Papaver rhoeas
Pelargonium (various varieties)
Penstemon barbatus
Petunia 'Red Star'; P. 'Scarlet'
Tropaeolum majus 'Empress of India'
Verbena (various varieties)

RED

The fiery reds are hot, exciting colours. They combine well with oranges, and golden and orange-yellows, but don't generally mix well with blue-reds, which are more sub-dued. Use them wherever you want to inject some vibrancy into your garden designs – in beds and borders or in hanging baskets and other containers. But remember that too much of a good thing can become monotonous, so use these strong colours sparingly.

Hot reds can be found in many perennials, but are especially well represented in summer annuals, which are so useful for adding dramatic patches of colour between other plants.

11

Above: This brilliant bright orange Osteospermum *makes a strong contrast against green foliage.*

ORANGE

A warm, friendly colour, orange has quite a wide range of shades. At the deeper end of the spectrum it is quite definitely a hot colour, exciting and vibrant, but at the golden end it is warm rather than hot and can be used more freely.

Orange mixes well with most colours although the redder shades are not so complementary with the bluer reds, including purple and pink, unless you like to combine colours that clash. It shows up well against green foliage and can be picked out at a distance.

Autumn gardens often display orange tones, not only in flowers, such as chrysanthemums, but in trees and shrubs with coloured foliage and brightly coloured berries.

ORANGE FLOWERS

Antirrhinum
Canna 'Orange Perfection'
Crocosmia
Dahlia
Eccremocarpus scaber
Erysimum
Euphorbia griffithii
Geum 'Borisii'
Hemerocallis
Kniphofia
Ligularia
Papaver orientale
Potentilla 'William Robinson'
Primula bulleyana
Rudbeckia hirta
Tagetes erecta
Tropaeolum
Trollius
Zauschneria californica

Above: This Calceolaria, *with its flame-orange flowers, is a striking annual to use in the border.*

Many annuals and biennials can add a vibrant orange note throughout the year, including winter-flowering pansies followed by wallflowers (*Erysimum*), snapdragons (*Antirrhinum*) and pot marigolds (*Calendula*). During summer, nasturtiums (*Tropaeolum*) and African marigolds (*Tagetes erecta*) will follow.

YELLOW

There are three distinct yellows within this part of the spectrum, all exhibiting different qualities in a planting scheme. One side is tinged with green and may be described as a cool colour, while the other side is tinged with orange, making it very much a hot colour. These hot yellows have a warm, cosy feeling about them, and go well with flame-reds, oranges and creams. In

Above: The yellow heads of Achillea *'Coronation Gold' float above its delicate foliage.*

between the two yellows are pure clear yellows. These will blend happily with most other colours.

The green or lemon yellows look much better when associated with greens blues and white. They can be bright, but create a fresher effect than the warmer yellows.

Above: The stately yellow spires of Verbascum *add height to a traditional summer border.*

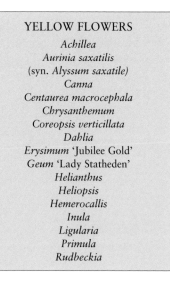

YELLOW FLOWERS

Achillea
Aurinia saxatilis
(syn. *Alyssum saxatile*)
Canna
Centaurea macrocephala
Chrysanthemum
Coreopsis verticillata
Dahlia
Erysimum 'Jubilee Gold'
Geum 'Lady Statheden'
Helianthus
Heliopsis
Hemerocallis
Inula
Ligularia
Primula
Rudbeckia

GREEN

Foliage can provide an effective link in borders and beds. Dark green is good used with hot colours, whereas soft green and silver suit cool colours, especially pink, pale blue and pale, greeny yellow. Blue foliage, which can be found in some grasses and hostas, can also be useful in linking or separating blocks of colour.

BLUE

The different shades of blue can be bright, clean-cut colours with a great intensity, or softened to such an extent that they only have a whisper of colour left, creating a very soft, hazy image. Intense blues can be used in a bold way in the garden, but the softer blues are good for romantic container arrangements, especially those in large stone pots or urns.

Above: Use the delicate Nigella damascena, *with its blue flowers and feathery fronds, in a cool border.*

Blues are versatile and can be combined with most colours. They create a rather rich, luxurious combination with purple-reds, but avoid mixing them with orange-reds. With orange, however, the effects can be startling, so use this combination sparingly.

Blue and yellow is another exciting combination, giving a fresh, clean-looking contrast. The pale blues and yellows, however, are more hazy and have a soft, romantic image, but still retain a distinctive, fresh quality.

Blues set against silver or grey foliage create an interesting combination that is distinct yet soft.

PURPLE AND VIOLET

Even a patch of purple appears as a strong block of colour, never as a misty haze. Over-use of this solid colour can have a deadening effect. As purple

---

BLUE FLOWERS

Agapanthus praecoc x subsp *orientalis*
Ageratum houstonianum
Brachyscome iberidifolia
Campanula medium
Centaurea cyanus
Consolida ambigua
Eryngium x *oliverianum*
Felicia bergeriana
Lathyrus odoratus
Limonium sinuatum 'Blue Bonnet'
Lobelia erinus
Myosotis
Nigella damascena
Nolana paradoxa 'Blue Bird'
Salvia farinacea 'Victoria'

Above: Digitalis *creates wonderfully elegant spires of flowers, bringing height to a planting scheme. These flowers vary in colour from a light pink to purple.*

too much, creating a leaden effect. Lime-green flowers such as lime zinnias and the lime foliage of *Helychrysum petiolare* 'Limelight' make excellent border companions.

Lavenders combined with pinks are a delightfully romantic combination and have the bonus of a delightful scent. When used with creamy-yellow they have a soothing effect.

PINK

This colour can be quite bright, even startling and brash, particularly when tinged with purple and moving towards cerise and magenta shades. On the other hand it can be very soft and romantic. You have to be careful

tends to sink back into green foliage, it is better to contrast it with foliage that is silver or grey.

Violet is a more lively colour, and has still more vibrancy when on the dark side. Nonetheless, it should still be used with care and discretion.

Both purple and violet can be used more extensively if they are mixed with other colours. Lighter colours, such as yellows and whites, contrast with and stand out against purple. Purple also harmonizes well with purple-reds and purple-blues, but if these are too dark, the colours tend to blend

Above: The delicate pink flowers of Olenothera speciosa rosea *have creamy white centres.*

PINK FLOWERS
Anemone hupehensis
Astilbe x *arendsii* 'Venus'
Centaurea Cyanus
Cleome hasslerianna 'Colour Fountain'
Cosmos bipinnatus 'Sensation'
Dicentra spectabilis
Geranium x *oxonianum*
'Wargrave Pink'
Impatiens
Lathyrus odoratus
Matthiola, Brompton Series
Penstemon
Petunia, Resisto Series

Above: *Cream blended with soft mauve and gently variegated foliage creates a soothing effect.*

in choosing the right colour for the effect you want to achieve. Pinks tend to mix best with lavenders and soft blues. But they can be used with reds to tone them down slightly. Pinks do not mix harmoniously with bright yellows and oranges.

CREAM
White mixed with a little yellow makes the sensuous and luxurious shade of cream. It goes well with most

colours, adding a slightly mellow hue and often blending in sympathetically with hot colours.

WHITE
Long associated with purity, peace and tranquillity, white flowers add sophistication to a scheme. White goes well with most other colours, and it can be used to lighten a colour scheme. Used with hot oranges and reds, pure white can create a dramatic effect. White and blue is always a popular combination and it can be particularly effective to combine different shades of white with a mixture of pastel colours.

White is visible until well after dark, and so it is a good colour to plant where you eat evening meals. It also can be used to illuminate dark

Left: *The large pompom heads of creamy yellow* Marigold *'French Vanilla'.*

16

corners of the garden. White busy Lizzies (*Impatiens*), for example, in a hanging basket against a dark background or in shade, will shine out.

A disadvantage with white flowers is that they often look unsightly when they die. To keep such displays at their best, deadhead once a day.

Some gardeners devote whole borders, even whole gardens, to white flowers. Although these are referred to as white gardens, there are usually at least two colours present, because most white-flowered plants have green leaves. A third colour, in the form of grey or silver foliage, is also often added.

There are many different shades of white, and they do not always mix sympathetically. On the whole, therefore, it is better to plant pure whites since the creamier ones tend to "muddy" the picture. Many white and cream flowers have bright yellow centres, and it is best to avoid these if you are planning a white border.

Above: The tiny flowers of Gypsophila elegans *make a delicate display in any summer border.*

WHITE FLOWERS

Alcea rosea
Anaphalis margaritacea
Clarkia pulchella 'Snowflake'
Cosmos bipinnatus 'Purity'
Gypsophila elegans 'Giant White'
Impatiens 'Super Elfin White'
Lathyrus odoratus
Lobelia erinus 'Snowball'
Lobularia maritima
(syn. Alyssum maritimum)
Matthiola (white varieties)
Nicotiana alata
Osteospermum 'Glistening White'
Pelargonium (various white forms)
Petunia (various white forms)
Viola x *wittrockiana* (white varieties)

Left: This white Osteospermum *will lighten any scheme, from hot oranges to misty blues.*

Year-round Plants

BY SELECTING PLANTS WITH YEAR-ROUND INTEREST, IT IS POSSIBLE TO
ACHIEVE CONTINUOUS COLOUR WITH MINIMUM EFFORT. HEATHERS,
GRASSES AND EVERGREENS, INCLUDING CONIFERS AND IVIES, ARE
ALL INVALUABLE SOURCES OF RICH COLOUR.

Above: The genus Calluna *consists of one species,* C. vulgaris, *but this has over 500 cultivars in a wide range of colours.*

HEATHERS

Multi-coloured heathers are enduring garden performers. Tough and hardy, most can withstand extreme conditions, and some even put on their finest performance when the weather is at its most severe. One of the many advantages of heathers is that they provide year-round colour. Not only is there a heather in flower every month of the year, but some have coloured foliage that can itself be a strong, year-round feature, the leaf colour often changing with the seasons. For gardens without acid soil, many heathers need to be grown in raised beds or containers with the correct acidity.

Heathers are most highly rated as plants for the winter garden. Choose from varieties of *Erica carnea* and *E. x darleyensis*, perhaps mixing in selections of *Calluna vulgaris*.

COLOURFUL HEATHERS

Calluna vulgaris:
'Beoley Gold', golden-yellow
'Golden Feather', gold/orange red
'Multicolor', yellowish green, orange and coral tips
'Red Fred', dark green/vivid red tips
'Roland Haagen', gold/orange-red
'Sister Anne', grey-green/bronze
'Sunset', golden-yellow/orange/red

Erica:
E. carnea 'Ann Sparkes', golden-yellow, bronze tips
'Foxhollow', yellow/slightly orange
'Golden Starlet', lime-green/yellow
'Westwood Yellow', yellow
E. cinerea 'Fiddler's Gold', golden-yellow/red
'Lime Soda', lime green
'Windlebrooke', golden yellow/orange-red
E. x darleyensis
'J.W. Porter', red and cream tips
E. vagans 'Valerie Proudley', bright yellow

In summer, varieties of *Calluna vulgaris*, *Erica cinerea* and *E. vagans* dominate the scene, and are all effective with other acid-loving plants.

As an edging to a shrub border, heathers provide a softer line than the more conventional *Buxus sempervirens*.

GRASSES

A wide variety of ornamental grasses is available, ensuring that there is usually at least one type for every garden situation. Grasses look good when grouped together, or used as single specimens. They often work particularly well when associated with other plants. Their airy form and movement contrast effectively with larger-leaved plants, and their vertical accent lifts and lightens dense groupings. They are particularly useful for adding winter interest.

Above: A collection of grasses in containers makes a versatile display for a small garden terrace or balcony.

In shady areas, the variegated foliage of *Carex hachijoensis* 'Evergold' will shine out all year round. Other shade-tolerant variegated grasses include *Molinia caerulea* ssp. *caerula* 'Variegata', *Hakonechloa macra* 'Alboaurea' and 'Aureola' and *Phalaris arundinacea* var. *picta* 'Picta'. They complement other shade-loving plants such as hostas, ferns and hydrangeas.

Areas of dry shade are difficult to plant successfully but *Stipa arundinacea* copes with these inhospitable conditions. Shady woodland areas can be carpeted with the golden foliage of *Milium effusum* 'Aureum', or with varieties of *Deschampsia cespitosa*, which have elegant flower spikes that catch the light beautifully.

Left: Use grasses, such as this Stipa calamagrostis, *as architectural plants in your scheme.*

EVERGREENS

Brachyglottis (Dunedin Group)
'Sunshine'
Choisya
Daphne tangutica
Euonymus fortunei
Hebe cupressoides
Ligustrum lucidum
Pieris japonica
Rhododendron
Santolina chamaecyparis
Vinca

Above: Many of the hebes are evergreen. This one, H. cupressoides, has striking violet flowers and small leaves.

EVERGREENS

The great feature of evergreens is that they hold on to their leaves throughout the year. They can be used as a permanent part of the structure of any border or garden. Unless they are carefully sited, however, evergreens can become a bit dull, so plan your planting with care.

Many evergreens have dark green leaves, but using plants with variegated leaves, or clever planting combinations, will add colour and interest. Try *Eleagnus pungens* 'Maculata' with its yellow-centred leaves or *Ligustrum lucidum* 'Excelsior Superbum', which has a golden variegation in the open, although in shade it glows with a bright yellowish green.

Lots of evergreens have the bonus of glorious flowers. Rhododendrons and azaleas in particular, many of the evergreen hebes and camellias, are prized for their gorgeously coloured blooms. *Choisya* is a good example.

The shiny leaves catch the sun and it produces masses of fragrant white flowers in spring and often again later in the year.

CONIFERS

Dwarf conifers are especially useful for providing year-round interest. Planted close together they will grow into each other, assuming a sculptural quality, besides making excellent ground cover. Some form dense mats,

DWARF CONIFERS

Abies Cephalonica 'Meyer's Dwarf'
Chamaecyparis lawsoniana
'Minima Aurea'
Juniperus communis 'Compressa'
Taxus baccuta 'Elegantissima'
Thuja orientalis 'Aurea Nana'
Thuja plicata 'Irish Gold'
Picea glauca var. *albertiana* 'Conica'
Picea pungens 'Globosa'

Above: Conifers provide a wonderful selection of shapes and textures. This juniper produces an attractive "sea of waves" effect that can never become boring.

IVIES
Hedera 'Bruder Ingobert'
Hedera helix 'Goldheart'
Hedera hibernica
Hedera 'Merion Beauty'

edged, gold-centred leaves, retains its colour on a shaded wall. Don't grow different ivies too closely together on walls or they will cover each other.

Some designers use mixed ivies for mass bedding, but these do require pruning once or twice a year. Ivy also makes excellent edging to a flower border. It can be grown along the edge of a garden path or planted on a terrace garden to great effect.

Ivies make excellent ground cover and can completely cover large areas quickly. One of the best for this is *Hedera hibernica*. Many *Hedera helix* cultivars are also suitable, especially the dark green 'Ivalace' or 'Shamrock'.

particularly the prostrate junipers such as *Juniperus horizontalis*, *J squamata* and *J. procumbens*.

Most dwarf conifers are suitable for rock gardens and containers, and also look good planted with heathers. Choose upright conifers, to provide height.

Ivies

One of the great features of ivies is their ability to cover and conceal unsightly structures or eyesores. They will thrive in different locations.

The classic situation for ivy is growing up a wall. *Hedera helix* 'Buttercup' is spectacular against a sunny wall. *H. h.* 'Goldheart', which has green-

Above: Here a golden ivy rambles happily over a wall intermingled with a rose and underplanted with complementary flowers.

Spring

Freshness and vitality are the keynotes of spring. Foliage and flowers are brightly coloured, with sunny yellow one of the most prevalent colours.

Plants at their Best

After the short, dark days of winter, spring begins tentatively with a few jewel-coloured bulbs and occasional perennial flowers. Flower buds on trees and shrubs begin to open. Before long plants are bursting into colour all around. The spring light makes everything in the garden look new and fresh.

Bulbs

This is a wonderful season for bulbs and corms of all kinds. There is a multitude of crocuses, daffodils, tulips, hyacinths, fritillaries, dog's tooth violet (*Erythronium*), irises, snowflake (*Leucojum*), grape hyacinths and trilliums, coming into flower in grass, borders and containers. These are all hardy plants, unharmed by frosts.

Above: Spring in the cottage garden is a glorious jumble of colours with primulas, Myosotis *(forget-me-nots) and* Dicentra.

Perennials

Some herbaceous plants have been around all winter. Lungworts (*Pulmonaria*), for example, have been in full leaf constantly, but now produce masses of blue, red, pink or white flowers. Hellebores are flowering as are primulas, of which the primrose is perhaps the best loved. As the days continue to lengthen and the air and ground become warmer, early flowers move into the background as other herbaceous perennials begin to emerge. Among the next phase are bleeding hearts (*Dicentra spectabilis*) and other dicentras, which need light shade and

Left: Hyacinthus orientalis *'Pink Pearl' interspersed with* Viola *makes a beautiful, scented display.*

will grow happily under trees that have yet to open their leaves. Wood anemones (*Anemone nemorosa*), in a range of white and delicate blues, pinks and yellow, also make use of the temporary light under deciduous trees and shrubs. Among the brightest flowers are the brilliant golden daisies of leopard's bane (*Doronicum*), and buttery kingcup (*Caltha*) flowers, which are essential for any bog or waterside planting. *Paeonia mlokosewitschii*, one of the earliest peonies to flower, has delicate yellow flowers.

Shrubs

Many shrubs flower early in the year. Rhododendrons, azaleas, magnolias, pieris, camellias and many others provide outstanding spring colour.

Spiraea 'Arguta' is among the earliest to flower, producing frothy pure white flowers over quite a long period. One of the best-loved shrubs is *Magnolia stellata* with its mass of delicate, star-like flowers in glistening

Above: Euphorbia polychroma *creates a perfect dome which is effective in any spring border.*

white or tinged with pink. The effect is enhanced because the flowers appear before the leaves develop. *Exochorda* x *macrantha* 'The Bride' is so covered in pure white flowers that the leaves are barely visible.

Forsythia creates one of the biggest splashes of spring colour. It should be cut back immediately after flowering to ensure that new flowering shoots grow in time for next season. Lilac (*Syringa*), prized for its colour and perfume, flowers late in the season. The white forms especially can look untidy when the flowers die, so they should be removed.

Rhododendrons and azaleas, especially, have such a vast range of glorious colours and flower sizes, that perhaps the best way to make a choice for your own garden is to see as many as you can in flower and then discover the names of the ones you like.

Left: Rhododendrons grow into large shrubs *which burst into colour in late spring.*

Colour Combinations

In lawns and under shrubs and trees, naturalized bulbs flower in cheerful multi-coloured carpets without constraint. In many spring borders, however, regularity and uniformity of planting are often preferred. Spring light has a softening effect and so strong opposing colours, such as primary red and blue, seem to go together better at this time of year.

Formal Beds

In formal beds you can interplant spring bulbs with bushy bedding plants, for example late-flowering tulips with pansies, forget-me-nots, polyanthus, double daisies *(Bellis perennis)* or dwarf wallflowers. These bedding plants hide the bare soil and make tall-stemmed bulbs like tulips less ungainly and vulnerable to wind damage. Pink tulips with blue forget-me-nots is a classic combination that can be enlivened by the occasional dot of a red tulip.

Such schemes offer scope for colour coordination and combinations that vary from the subtle to the gaudy. For example, pale pink hyacinths and white or pale yellow *Polyanthus* make a restful, receding combination, while deep yellow *Polyanthus* makes an arresting sight. Try planting two different kinds of spring bulbs together, such as bright blue *Scilla siberica* among 'Pink Pearl' hyacinths.

Such a border, recreated at the home of Monet in Giverney, France, combines a number of favourites – tall bearded blue-and-white iris fronting masses of Siberian wallflowers (*Erysimum hieracaciifolium*), scented wallflowers and *Hesperis matronalis*. All of this display could be edged with purple-flowered *Lobularia maritima* 'Royal Carpet'.

Informal Borders

Planting an informal border is easier. Generally, bold clumps of a single variety work best in a border, and if the clumps or drifts are used to fill gaps they will probably be well spaced out with little risk of colour clashes. It is often possible to plant bulbs between perennials that will hide the dying foliage as they emerge.

Above: The variegated Weigela florida *'Albomarginata' is seen here against a* Spiraea. *The striped leaves blend well with the white flowers of the* Spiraea *in spring.*

Above: Dainty yellow primroses are charmingly set off by their own green foliage and enhanced by a fountain of yellow grass.

NATURAL EFFECT

For a natural effect in borders, try a mass planting of spring-flowering bulbs and perennials. Purple crocus and yellow aconites could be planted to flower above the marbled leaves of *Arum italicum pictum*, with the rich mauve flowers of hellebores atop leafless stems. Around these could perhaps be scattered the green-tipped white bells of snowdrops.

The strong blue of grape hyacinths with the pale yellow of primroses is another time-honoured spring combination. Or you could try a mix of hyacinths, compact tulips and narcissi. Planted closely for maximum impact, these would be as colourful as any summer bedding.

PLANTS AT THEIR BEST
EARLY SPRING

Bergenia (non-woody evergreen)
Camellia (shrub)
Crocus (bulb)
Eranthis hyemalis (bulb)
Helleborus orientalis (perennial)
Hyacinthus (bulb)
Iris reticulata (bulb)
Magnolia stellata (shrub)
Primula x *polyantha* (perennial)
Tulipa kaufmanniana (bulb)

MID-SPRING

Amelanchier (shrub/tree)
Cytisus, various (shrub)
Dicentra (perennial)
Doronicum (perennial)
Magnolia x *soulangiana* (tree)
Magnolia stellata (shrub)
Narcissus (bulb)
Prunus 'Kwanzan' (tree)
Rhododendron, various (shrub)
Ribes sanguineum (shrub)

LATE SPRING

Azalea (shrub)
Bergenia (non-woody evergreen)
Cheiranthus (wallflower)
Choisya ternata (shrub)
Clematis montana (shrubby climber)
Cytisus, various (shrub)
Dicentra (perennial)
Fritillaria (bulb)
Laburnum (tree)
Malus (tree)
Paeonia (perennial and shrub)
Phlox subulata (rock plant)
Pulsatilla vulgaris (rock plant)
Rhododendron, various (shrub)
Saxifraga, various (rock plant)
Syringa (shrub)
Tulipa, various (bulb)
Wisteria (shrubby climber)

Jobs to Do

In cold regions the weather can still be icy in early spring, but in mild climates you can make a start on many outdoor jobs, including feeding and mulching beds and borders, and spring-pruning shrubs if applicable. If sowing or planting outdoors, bear in mind that soil and air temperature are important. Few seeds will germinate if the soil temperature is below 7°C (45°F), so use a soil thermometer to check before you sow.

By mid-spring, outdoor sowing and planting can begin in earnest. You can plant container-grown shrubs, herbaceous perennials, gladioli and other summer bulbs and tubers, as well as making a start on sowing hardy annuals. Plants sown or planted in late spring often catch up with those sown a month earlier if the weather was unseasonably cold.

Late spring can be deceptive, and in cold areas late frosts can occur. Take local climate into account before planting any frost-tender plants outdoors or hardening off tender bedding plants. Watch to see when summer bedding is put out in local parks, by gardeners with local knowledge.

Prune spring-flowering shrubs, such as *Ribes sanguineum* and forsythia immediately they finish flowering. At the end of the season, you can start planting up hanging baskets and containers for summer displays.

Harden off Bedding Plants

It is crucial for all plants raised indoors or in a greenhouse to be hardened off. This gradually accustoms cosseted plants to withstand the harsher conditions outdoors. Place the plants in a cold frame a week or two before planting out. Close the top in the evening and on cold days, otherwise ventilate freely. If a sharp frost threatens, cover the frame with insulation material, such as bubble polythene.

Below: By late spring you can plant up your hanging baskets for a summer display like this.

POT UP AND POT ON CUTTINGS

1 Pot up pelargonium and fuchsia cuttings that were made the previous summer, as soon as they have formed strong root growth. Use an 8–10cm (3–4in) pot and a potting compost (soil mix) suitable for young plants. Water thoroughly, then keep out of direct sunlight for a couple of days while they recover.

2 Cuttings that rooted earlier and have already been potted up for a month or more may need moving into larger pots. Move only if the roots have filled the pot.

3 Use a pot a couple of sizes larger and trickle the same kind of potting compost around the roots. Firm well and water.

TAKE SOFTWOOD CUTTINGS

1 In mid-spring take softwood cuttings of fuchsias below the third or fourth leaf or pair of leaves. Pot up and cover with a plastic bag that does not touch the leaves.

ENCOURAGE BUSHY FUCHSIAS

1 Bush-shaped fuchsias respond well to early "pruning" and training. Pinch out the growing tip as soon as the cuttings have three pairs of leaves.

2 New shoots will form after a few weeks, but for really bushy plants, pinch out the tips of these side shoots too. Repeat this process several times during spring to encourage well-shaped bushy plants.

PRICK OUT SEEDLINGS

1 Prick out seedlings as soon as they are large enough to handle. Choose a module that suits the size of plant. Fill the individual cells loosely with a potting compost (soil mix) suitable for seedlings.

2 Strike the compost off level with the top of the module using a straight-edge, but do not compress. It will settle lower once the seedlings have been inserted and watered.

3 Loosen the seedlings and, if possible, lift one at a time by their seed leaves. These are the first to open, and are usually smaller and a different shape from the true leaves. Do not lift them by the stems as these are very fragile.

4 Using a small tool, make a hole in each cell that is large enough to take the roots of the seedlings with as little damage to them as possible. Gently firm the compost around the roots, without pressing. Water the seedlings thoroughly, then keep in shade for a few days.

PRICK OUT INTO POTS

There are a few special cases when more than a single seedling is used because they are too small to handle individually. For example, lobelias have seedlings that are tiny, and the individual plants are not very substantial when they are mature, so many gardeners choose to prick out a small group of seedlings, about five or six, together. By the time these have grown into seedlings that are large enough to plant out they look like one substantial plant.

Above: Scarlet Verbena *plants that were sown as seeds in the spring.*

PLANT A HANGING BASKET

1 Stand the basket on a large pot or a bucket to keep it stable while planting. Use a wire basket if you want a traditional display with plenty of plants cascading from the sides as well as the top. Include trailing plants such as *Lobelia erinus* in your selection.

2 You can use a proprietary liner and make slits for planting, but if you are making a traditional basket, line it with moss to the level of the first row of plants. Fill the basket with potting compost (soil mix) up to that level, then insert the plants.

3 Add more moss and potting compost and repeat until just below the rim. Use a bold plant for the centre. You may need to remove a little of the potting compost from the root-ball (roots) if the plant has been in a large pot.

4 Finally, fill in with a selection of plants around the edges. Encourage cascading plants to trail quickly and effectively by planting the root-ball at a slight angle so that the plant tilts slightly towards the edge of the basket.

Left: A thoughtfully planted hanging basket will flower throughout the summer and into the early autumn.

29

Summer

Plants at Their Best

Although often regarded as a continuation in gardening terms there is quite a difference between early, mid- and late summer.

Early summer carries on where spring left off, with plenty of fresh-looking foliage and bright, rich colours. Lupins, poppies, peonies and delphiniums are vital players in any display at this time of the year.

As midsummer approaches, the colours change subtly and flowers with more muted tones unfurl. Among these are *Phlox*, *Catanache* (sometimes known as Cupid's dart), penstemons and *Gypsophila*.

By late summer colours are fading and foliage is starting to look a little tired. Autumnal tones become evident with the deep golds and russet-reds of perennials such as achilleas, heleniums and inulas.

Perennials

Summer is the height of the perennial year. The hardy geraniums (pelargoniums) are one of the mainstays of the summer border. There is a vast range to choose from.

Above: A variety of different shades of yellow are broken up by contrasting splashes of red in this summer garden.

Pelargoniums are widely grown for the visual impact of their flowers and for their coloured foliage. They can be grown in borders, or in containers.

Dahlias are useful for borders as they last for months, come in many different heights and provide lots of flowers for cutting.

Tuberous-rooted begonias, used for both bedding and container display, come in shades of pink, red, yellow and white. Seed-raised begonias that flower quickly, such as Non-stop, are also popular. They flower all summer,

30

until cut back by frost, and are suitable for massed bedding. These are all low growing, reaching 23–30cm (9–12in) in height.

The tall – up to 1.8m (6ft) – exotic-looking cannas come into bloom early and continue until the first frost. They combine spectacular red, orange or yellow flowers with interesting foliage, mostly dark or purple bronze but some brightly variegated.

Bulbs

Summer-flowering bulbs are exceptionally good for adding highlights to a traditional herbaceous border, and can be useful for brightening up areas between shrubs that have finished flowering. It is difficult to imagine a traditional herbaceous border, for example, without groups of lilies or a clump or two of crocosmias. The crocosmia corms multiply freely, and after a year or two most plantings

Above: The pink globes of Allium christophii *contrast successfully with* Salvia sylvestris.

Above: Yellow achillea and the streaked leaves of Canna 'Striata' *make an effective backdrop for* Crocosmia 'Lucifer'.

make a bold show in late summer with arching sprays of red, orange or yellow flowers.

The round, colourful heads of alliums make stunning statements in the summer border. There are many forms including dwarf ones like the yellow *Allium moly*, *A. christophii*, with its 15cm (6in) spheres of starry, lilac flowers, and tall, majestic species such as the 1.8m (6ft) *A. giganteum* with its huge bloom. *A. sphaerocephalon* has drumstick heads of pinkish-purple flowers on thin 75cm (2½ft) tall stems. It is best grown mid-border, where other border plants can hide and support the stems. The seedheads are another delight. They can be enjoyed in the garden or used indoors in dried flower arrangements.

Shrubs

From midsummer onwards, many shrubs begin to flower. These include brightly flowering shrubs such as *Hypericum calycinum*, which, with its brilliant yellow flowers, will even flourish in shade. For a sunny spot, the bright pinks and oranges of helianthemums, or the soft-pink shades of *Cistus* are a delight. Use white-flowering shrubs such as *Cistus laurifolius* or *Philadelphus* to break up bold masses of colour and act as a backdrop to vivid shades.

Hydrangeas, with their huge mounds of blooms, prefer shady positions, where the whites will brighten up their surroundings. The delicate lacecaps are popular because of the shape of the flowers. *Hydrangea quercifolia*

Above: The glorious cascading flowers of Fuchsia 'Cotton Candy' would be a delightful addition to the summer scheme.

Above: A white Hydrangea thrives in a shaded border.

combines white flowers, which become tinged pink with age, with mid-green leaves which will turn bronze in autumn. *H. aspera* 'Villosa' has mauvish-blue and pink flowers. Mophead varieties (*H. macrophylla*) bear blue flowers on acid soil, red ones on neutral soil and pink ones on alkaline soil.

Few other plants smother themselves so completely or over such a long period as fuchsias. Ranging from almost white, through pastel pink to rich purples, reds and oranges, the flower shapes and colours of fuchsias offer unlimited possibilities. Tender types have become prized bedding plants, while the often less showy hardy types can be integrated into mixed borders, where they can give years of pleasure. Some hardy fuchsias

Above: Clematis *'Purpurea Plena Elegans'* provides the interest now that its host plant, Rosa *'Cécile Brünner, climbing'*, has all but finished flowering.

make elegant plants that can stand alone as specimens in a bed or in a suitable container.

Roses are at their best in summer. Some are once-flowering and do so in the early summer, but many go on flowering throughout the whole season. Some gardeners prefer to have a separate garden or special beds for roses, while others like to mix them in with other plants.

Climbers

Interesting effects can be created using climbing roses. The rambling 'Albertine', for example, can be grown to produce a glorious fountain of salmon-pink flowers up to 6m (20ft) high.

Like climbing roses, clematis can be grown in a variety of ways, on pergolas, against walls and fences. The more vigorous types will reach into trees to provide glorious colour and height. There are many startling colours to choose from, ranging from deep rose-pink through crimson and wine red to bright purple, in small or large flower sizes. You can select from the three different groups to ensure colour throughout the summer.

PLANTS AT THEIR BEST

EARLY SUMMER

Allium
Dianthus
Geranium
Iris germanica hybrids
Paeonia
Papaver orientale
Philadelphus

MID-SUMMER

Clematis
Digitalis
Geranium
Hardy annuals
Hydrangea
Hypericum
Lavandula
Lilium
Rosa

LATE SUMMER

Dahlia
Fuchsia
Helenium
Hibiscus syriacus
Hypericum
Lavatera
Perovskia atriplicifolia
Romneya
Solidago
Summer bedding

Above: Orange and blue are both powerful colours. Used together in a planting scheme, they produce an agreeable tension as is shown by the bright Agapanthus *and orange* Crocosmia.

COLOUR COMBINATIONS

With all the colour that is around during summer, some stunning plantings are possible.

Beds and Borders

At this time of year blues can be tinged with pink, making them work well with mauves and violets. For example, *Echium* 'Blue Bedder', which comes in varying shades of blue, combines beautifully with *Penstemon* 'Sour Grapes'. To create a restful mood, try fronting spires of purplish-blue delphiniums with a mass of violet-blue *Geranium ibericum*.

Including white flowers in a planting with a lot of soft blues and pinks will soothe the whole effect; blue and

pink with occasional pure white highlights is a favourite scheme for the summer border.

While some gardeners will relish a totally hot composition, most will want to use red with some discretion at this time of the year. Even a combination of bright red and blue, achieved perhaps by planting red oriental poppies with blue anchusas, can be too strong for some. If you prefer a pink-and-pastel summer mix, do include the occasional hot red such as *Penstemon*, *Kniphofia* or *Crocosmia* to add some spice.

Above: The stunning white bloom of the Easter or Bermuda Lily (L. longiflorium).

A White Border

Cool white summer plantings can be centred on white lilies, perhaps combining them with 'Iceberg' roses, hazy *Gypsophila* and white *Penstemon*. Lilies make a good focal point in the border, and will flower above a sea of

Above: The glorious white flowers of Rosa 'Madame Hardy' *will enhance a traditional cottage garden.*

herbaceous plants. The Madonna Lily *(Lilium candidum)* is a traditional cottage garden plant that blends well with old-fashioned roses. You could fill out such a scheme with *Hebe rakaiensis* and grey-green leaved *Anaphalis triplinervis*, both white flowered. You could also include silvery-leaved plants.

Effects with Climbers

The evergreen foliage of the many types of conifers provides a superb foil for the bright blooms of summer-flowering climbers. Climbers can also be allowed to scramble through formally trained plants, creating different effects. Mixing violet-blue *Clematis* 'Ascotiensis' with the creamy white old-fashioned *Rosa* 'Albéric' Barbier, for instance, produces a cool, striking result and will provide colour over a long period.

Late-flowering clematis can be encouraged to meander through heathers. The less vigorous, small-flowered viticella or texensis types of clematis, in the same colour range as the heathers, are best for this purpose (summer-flowering species would be too rampant). The flowers of *Clematis* 'Royal Velours' glow like rubies against the velvety old-gold foliage of *Erica carnea* 'Foxhollow', for instance. If you plant a clematis among winter-flowering *Erica*, however, you will have to cut it back in late autumn rather than late winter, as is generally recommended, so that the clematis does not smother the heather flowers. Clematis can also be grown up small trees to add interest to the lower section, which is without leaves.

Above: Climbers planted together prolong the colour in an area. Here Rosa 'Iceberg' *is grown with* Clematis tangutica.

Jobs to Do

Many of the planting and sowing jobs begun in spring can be completed during early summer – planting hanging baskets and containers, sowing hardy annuals and planting perennials, bulbs and tubers. Now is the time to sow biennials such as wallflowers and forget-me-nots and plant out any tender bedding plants.

As the display changes through the summer, it is important that the beds and borders are kept tidy and well-maintained. The flowers of each plant should be dead-headed as soon as they go over. This not only removes an eyesore, but also prevents the plant's energy from being spent on seed production. Instead, the energy is channelled back into the plant, which may then produce a second, later show of flowers.

Above: Disbud chrysanthemums if you want larger flowers later.

Some perennials benefit from being cut right back to the ground, which encourages a flush of new leaves, so they can then act as foliage plants. Lady's mantle (*Alchemilla mollis*), for example, not only looks tired and tatty if it is left, but it also seeds itself everywhere. If it is sheared back to its base after flowering, however, it will produce a set of beautiful new foliage and self-sowing will have been prevented.

Summer is the time to take semi-ripe cuttings, layer shrubs and carnations and move biennial and perennial seedlings to a nursery bed. As the season draws to a close, start planting spring bulbs and divide and replant irises.

Left: Dead-head lilacs as soon as they have finished flowering to prevent the tree's energy going into seed production.

SOW BIENNIALS AND HARDY PERENNIALS

1 Prepare the ground thoroughly, and eliminate as many weeds as possible. Competition from weeds is often the greatest enemy the seedlings face. Break the soil down into a fine, crumbly structure once it has been cleared of weeds.

3 Run water into the drill before sowing if the soil is very dry. Space the seeds thinly, and as evenly as you can. This will make thinning and transplanting much easier. A small dispenser tool is available from garden centres to make the task easier.

2 Take out a drill with the corner of a hoe or rake to the recommended depth (following the instructions on the seed packet). The drills can be quite close together.

4 Cover the seeds by shuffling the soil back with your feet or carefully ease the soil over with the back of a rake. Remember to add a label.

GARDENER'S TIP

In dry weather do not water the drill after sowing as this will cause the soil to harden, preventing germination of the seedlings.

5 Thin the seedlings as soon as they are large enough to handle easily so that they do not become overcrowded. Gently firm the soil around the seedlings that remain in the ground.

TAKE SEMI-RIPE CUTTINGS

1 Choose shoots that are almost fully grown except for the soft tip. The base of the cutting should be hardening, even though the tip may still be soft. Most cuttings are best made 5–10cm (2–4in) long.

2 Strip the lower leaves from each cutting to leave a short length of clear stem to insert into the soil. Dip the cut end into rooting hormone powder, liquid or gel. If using powder, dip the ends into water first.

3 Put the cuttings into a shallow drill. Cuttings taken from hardy plants will root outside at this time of year, though they will perform better in a cold frame.

4 Firm the cuttings to ensure there are no large pockets of air, which might cause the new roots to dry out. Remember to insert a label, especially if you are rooting a number of different kinds of shrubs.

5 Water thoroughly. It is worth adding a fungicide to the water initially, to reduce the chance of the cuttings rotting. Make sure that the soil does not dry out.

SHRUBS TO PROPAGATE FROM SEMI-RIPE CUTTINGS

Buddleja
Camellia
Choisya
Fuchsia
Hebe
Hydrangea
Philadelphus
Pyracantha
Rosemary

Above: *Taking semi-ripe cuttings of shrubs such as fuchsias can multiply your stock at no extra cost.*

PLANT BULBS FOR THE SPRING

1 Fork over the ground before planting, and if the plants are to be left undisturbed for some years, try to incorporate plenty of organic material such as rotted garden compost (soil mix) or manure. Many bulbs like well-drained soil, but still benefit from plenty of organic material.

2 Avoid adding quick-acting fertilizers in the autumn. Instead rake a very slow-acting fertilizer such as bonemeal, into the surface, or apply it to the planting holes.

3 Where there is space and the plants will benefit from planting in an informal group or cluster, dig out a sufficiently wide hole about three times the depth of the bulb.

4 Space the bulbs so that they look like a natural clump. Use the spacing that is recommended on the packet as a guide. Wide spacing will allow for future growth and multiplication, but if you intend to lift the bulbs after flowering, much closer spacing will create a bolder display.

5 Draw soil back over the planted bulbs with a rake, being careful not to dislodge them in the process. Put a marker around the whole area where they have been planted so that you do not walk over the bulbs and crush tender shoots as they emerge.

GARDENER'S TIP

Most bulbs have a very obvious top and bottom, so knowing which way to plant them presents no difficulty. Others, especially tubers, can cause confusion because they lack an obvious growing point. If in doubt, just plant them on their side. The shoots will grow upwards and the roots downwards.

Autumn

AUTUMN MAY WELL SIGNIFY THE END OF SUMMER, BUT IT COMPENSATES WITH A FLUSH OF GLORIOUS COLOUR. WARM YELLOWS, BURNING ORANGES AND BRONZE, AND FIERY REDS AND PURPLES ARE NEVER BETTER THAN NOW.

PLANTS AT THEIR BEST

Mellowed by the slanting autumn light, colours at this time of year become more muted, but there are still plenty of bright flowers around. Additionally, the tints and hues of foliage, berries and other fruit make this season a celebration of reds and browns which glow in the light and bring a warmth to the garden.

Above: The foliage of an Acer *tree is at its best in the autumn.*

Bulbs

Autumn-flowering bulbs are a delight, with exotic dahlias and cannas vying for attention with strident colours and bold foliage. Nerines bear their large heads of frilly, bright pink, trumpet-shaped flowers. Colchicums are found in various shades of lilac, pink and white and will grow in borders or grass in sun or partial shade. Other autumn highlights include the sternbergias, with their bright yellow, crocus-like flowers and crinums, which produce a wonderful array of large, pink, funnel-shaped flowers.

Above: The magnificent autumn flowering bulb Crinum x powellii *is also known as the Cape Lily.*

The open, cup-shaped flowers of the kaffir lily (*Schizostylis coccinea*) are available in shades of pink or red.

Perennials

Many perennial plants run on into autumn from summer but true autumn has its own distinctive flora. Michaelmas daisies (*Aster*) are one of the mainstays of the season, as are chrysanthemums, while vibrantly coloured sedums are invaluable for attracting the last of the butterflies and bees.

Yellows, oranges and bronzes are plentiful, with coneflowers *(Rudbeckia)* and sunflowers *(Helianthus)* in full flower, but there are also deep purple ironweeds *(Vernonia)*. Lilyturf *(Liriope)* has blue spikes of flowers and is useful because it is one of the few autumn-flowering plants that will grow in shade.

Above: The autumn border will look glorious with a display of Aster x frikartii.

Shrubs

Fuchsias, buddlejas, hibiscus and hydrangeas all continue to bloom in autumn. One of the few true autumn-flowering shrubs is *Osmanthus heterophyllus*, with fragrant white flowers. *Ceratostigma willmottianum* has piercingly blue flowers that continue well into autumn and *Eucryphia glutinosa* bears glistening white flowers with a central boss of stamens.

Foliage and Berries

The true glory of autumn, of course, belongs to foliage. Paramount for autumn beauty are the acers, trees and shrubs, which have a stunning range of leaf shades. Berries and other fruit are an added bonus; they are attractive and supply birds and other animals with a valuable food resource.

Above: Many shrubs have stunning berries in the autumn. Here Pyracantha *is covered with glowing orange berries.*

Above: The red leaves of Acer palmatum *'sakazuki' make a fiery climax to the year.*

COLOUR COMBINATIONS

The abundance of plant material and vibrant colour in the garden during autumn can provide some stimulating effects. Autumn flower colours can be arranged to harmonize with the season's colourful berries and changing leaves.

Beds and Borders

Whilst daisy-like plants such as chrysanthemums, dendranthemas, asters and the yellow-flowered *Rudbeckia* 'Goldsturm' are the mainstay of autumn borders, there are other plants that can be utilized, too.

Daisy plants can be combined with late-flowering dazzlers such as the white-flowered *Anemone japonica* 'Honorine Jobert'. *Achillea ptarmica* 'The Pearl', also white flowered, and *Campanula lactiflora*, are also good choices to extend the late summer border well into autumn.

Sedums take on some glowing hues now. At the front of a border, the pink-mauve flowers of the iceplant *Sedum* x *spectabile* 'Brilliant' planted with an eye-catching daisy plant like *Dendranthema* 'Raquel' would provide a long period of strong colour. Hostas could be substituted for sedums to edge a border. *Hosta* 'Honeybells' and *H.* 'Green fountain' both provide particularly glowing foliage as well as useful flowers. *Cephalaria gigantea* would make a bold display at the back of the border.

CONTRASTING SHAPES

Some interesting effects can be engineered by planting contrasting shapes and textures together. The tall, slender

Above: The autumn-flowering succulent Sedum spectabile *is a seasonal highlight.*

Above: Cortaderia selloana *'Sunningdale Silver'* is at its most splendid in the autumn months.

PLANTS AT THEIR BEST

EARLY AUTUMN
Anemone japonica
Aster novae-angliae
Aster novi-belgii
Chrysanthemum, early-flowering garden type
Dahlia
Hibiscus syriacus
Pyracantha
Rudbeckia
Sedum spectabile
Solidago
Sternbergia lutea

MID-AUTUMN
Acer
Anemone japonica
Aster novi-belgii
Fothergilla
Liriope muscari
Schizostylis coccinea

LATE AUTUMN
Berberis
Cotoneaster
Fothergilla
Gentiana sino-ornata
Liriope muscari
Nerine bowdenii
Pernettya
Pyracantha

flower spikes of cannas, which rise above their spiralling oval leaves, often brilliantly coloured at this time of year, can be contrasted with the roundness of dahlia flowers. These range from the large open flowers of the single forms to the round, tight balls of the Pompon varieties.

Dahlias also make interesting associations with ornamental grasses. Plant them with grasses such as *Calamagrostis* x *acutifolia*, *Miscanthus sinensis* or *Cortaderia selloana* to create a graceful picture. Try placing the copper-orange spikes of *Canna* 'Wyoming' alongside *Dahlia* 'David Howard' together with the lilac-purple flowers of *Verbena bonariensis*.

Right: Autumn is renowned for the warm tones of its plants and foliage. Dahlia 'David Howard' has glowing flowers.

Jobs to Do

Now is the time to prepare for the following year. Plant lilies and spring-flowering bulbs. Sow hardy annuals if your climate is mild enough or you can provide winter protection. Take fuchsia, perlagonium and hardwood cuttings. Divide perennials that have become over large.

Clear away dead matter and dying plants regularly to keep the autumn border looking tidy and to ensure that flowering perennials are visible.

Before winter sets in, lift, clean and store gladioli and other tender bulbs, corms and tubers. As soon as dahlias have been blackened by the first frost, lift and store them too. Protect vulnerable plants that will remain in the garden over winter.

Above: Cover tender plants with horticultural fleece or bubble polythene to protect from sharp frosts and damaging winter wind. Secure well with stakes and tie twine or string around the circumference of the plant.

If you are planning a major replanting of a border, start preparing the soil in the autumn, especially if you are planting shrubs. The ground will still be warm from the summer sun and easier to dig. This will also give the ground an opportunity to weather, with worms taking nutrients below the surface, and any remaining weeds that reappear can be cleared before planting begins again the following spring.

Plant Lilies for Summer

1 Dig an area that will take at least four or five bulbs 20cm (8in) deep and mix in well-rotted manure or garden compost (soil mix). Add grit and a little bonemeal.

2 Place the bulbs about 15cm (6in) apart and deep enough to be covered with twice their depth of soil so that they are well anchored when fully grown.

3 Sprinkle more grit and coarse sand around the bulbs to deter slugs and reduce the risk of waterlogging. Place small canes to mark the lilies' position.

PLANTING BEDDING PLANTS FOR A SPRING DISPLAY

1 Fork over the ground after clearing summer bedding plants. Fertilizer is not normally needed, but apply slow-acting bonemeal after forking over and rake it in.

2 If you have raised the spring-flowering plants yourself, water them well about an hour before lifting them. Using a hand fork, carefully lift each plant with some soil.

3 Spring bedding plants bought from garden centres or nurseries are usually sold in trays or strips. These are disposable, so don't be afraid to break them.

4 Space the plants out on the surface, allowing for any bulbs before planting. Space the bulbs out in an irregular pattern then plant from the back or one end.

LIFT AND PROTECT CHRYSANTHEMUMS

1 Lift the roots before frosts begin. Trim the tops and any long roots, to keep a compact shape. Select a tray that will take the roots in one layer.

2 Position the roots on a layer of compost (soil mix) in a tray. Cover with 2.5cm (1in) of compost and keep just moist. Store in a cool, light place.

LIFT AND STORE PELARGONIUMS

1 Using a fork, lift pelargoniums that have finished flowering before the first frost if possible. Shake as much of the soil off the roots as you can.

2 Trim the longest roots back to 5–8cm (2–3in) long, to make potting up easier.

3 Half fill a large tray with soil or sowing compost (soil mix). Position the plants and add more compost to cover the roots. Water well initially, then only when the soil becomes almost dry.

4 If you want to overwinter on a sunny windowsill, you may prefer to use large pots that will be more convenient.

GARDENER'S TIP

A cool but frost-free garage is a sensible place to store overwintering bulbs, corms and tubers. Keep bulbs, corms and tubers where you can easily check them about once a month, to ensure they are all still sound. Any that start to rot must be removed immediately to safeguard the rest.

Above: By storing pelargoniums they will survive over the winter.

PLANT A POT-GROWN ROSE

1 Dig a hole large enough to contain the root-ball (roots). Fork in as much garden compost (soil mix) or rotted manure as possible. Break up compacted soil.

2 Place the rose in the hole and use a cane laid across the top of the hole to check that the bud union is positioned about 1.5cm (1in) below the soil level.

3 Replace the soil and firm gently with your feet to ensure the rose is planted firmly with no large air pockets, and so that the bush cannot be rocked by wind. Rake over and water thoroughly.

4 If the plant was unpruned when bought, cut back all the shoots to about 15–20cm (6–8in) above the ground.

OVERWINTER DAHLIAS

1 Lift dahlias, using a fork, once the first frosts have blackened the foliage. Avoid damaging the roots with the prongs of the fork.

2 Cut off the stem, leaving a stump 5cm (2in) long. Stand the tubers upside-down on a supported mesh to allow moisture to drain from the hollow stems. Keep in a dry, frost-free place for a few days, when the tubers should be dry enough to store.

3 Remove surplus soil, trim loose bits off the roots and shorten the stem to a short stump. Label each plant and pack in a well-insulated box with peat, vermiculite, wood shavings or crumpled newspaper. Store in a frost-free location.

Winter

GARDENS CAN BE FULL OF COLOUR AT THIS TIME OF YEAR. THERE IS PLENTY TO SEE AND ENJOY, FROM STRIKING STEMS AND FOLIAGE TO BRIGHT FLOWERS THAT WILL DISPEL THE WINTER GLOOM.

PLANTS AT THEIR BEST

Winter light shows up plants in relief. Silvers and greys are sympathetic to the season, and green takes on new importance. Many evergreen shrubs, especially those with shiny leaves, can look particularly good in the weak winter sunlight.

Bulbs

There are many dainty winter-flowering bulbs and corms, including snowdrop cultivars, winter aconites (*Eranthis hyemalis*), early crocuses, dwarf irises, tiny cyclamen and *Anemone blanda*. The earliest daffodils, such as *Narcissus* 'January Gold', are slightly taller.

Above: Winter aconites bring a touch of colour at the end of the year.

The Algerian iris (*Iris unguicularis*) starts flowering in late autumn and continues until early spring, whatever the weather. Its mauve or purple flowers are deliciously scented.

Perennials

Primroses (*Primula vulgaris*) often flower sporadically at this time of year, and sweet violets (*Viola odorata*) will flower in warm spots. Hellebores (*Helleborus*) are one of the mainstays of the perennial scene in winter.

Left: Clump-forming hellebores add colour and architectural interest in winter.

Above: Conifers retain their glowing colours throughout the winter.

Shrubs

Many shrubs provide plenty of interest during winter months. Winter jasmine (*Jasminum nudiflorum*) is truly a winter plant, flowering from the end of autumn through to early spring, untroubled by frost and snow. Jasmine stems taken indoors make attractive winter flower decorations.

Winter hazels (*Corylopsis*), with their lovely yellow catkins, also make excellent winter plants. Witch hazels (*Hamamelis*) produce curious flowers, resembling clusters of tiny ribbons. As well as being attractive, they have a prominent smell that fills the air. Several viburnums flower during winter. *Viburnum tinus* is evergreen and covered with flat heads of small white flowers throughout most of the winter and often right through into spring.

Coloured Stems

Some shrubs are prized for the colours of their bare stems in winter. When planted to catch the low winter sunshine, they make a wonderful display. Dogwoods (*Cornus*) are renowned for the beauty of their stems with colours ranging from red though to yellow. *C. alba* is scarlet. Vibrant *C. stolonifera* 'Flaviramea' has yellowish green bark. *Rubus* 'Golden Veil', which has bright yellow foliage in summer, sports white stems in winter.

Several of the willows (*Salix*) have beautiful winter stems, which bear distinctive catkins at the end of the season. *S. alba* produces some of the best coloured stems, but there are many other good species.

Above: Daphne burkwoodii has an intense scent as well as delightful pink flowers.

COLOUR COMBINATIONS

As colour is so precious at this time of year and valued in its own right, planting combinations seem to have less importance than during other seasons. Nonetheless there are some delightful associations to be enjoyed.

Brightening the Gloom

The early woodland bulbs and perennials naturally favour locations under bushes and trees where they enjoy precious sunshine before the newly-formed leafy canopy obstructs their light and they cease flowering.

Snowdrops (*Galanthus*) multiply quickly where they are growing, especially in their natural habitat in damp

Above: A welcome sight in the winter, Cyclamen coum *and snowdrops.*

woodland, and will eventually spread to carpet vast areas with white and green. In the garden, you can plant them under shrubs to create a similar, if scaled down, effect. Winter aconites (*Eranthis hyemalis*) grown this way provide welcome splashes of yellow, rather than white, in dark places.

Above: The bright red stems of Cornus *lighten a wintery scene when branches are bare.*

WINTER HEATHERS

(Shrubs marked * are best cut back hard each spring for their winter stem effect.)

*Berberis temolacia**
Cornus alba 'Sibirica'*
Cornus sanguinea 'Winter Beauty'*
Cornus stolonifera 'Flaviramea'*
Garrya elliptica
Hamamelis mollis
Mahonia x *media* 'Charity'
Prunus subhirtella 'Autumnalis'
Rubus thibetanus
Salix alba var. vitellina 'Britzensis'*
Salix irrorata
Viburnum x *bodnantense* 'Dawn'
Viburnum tinus

Above: Heather can be relied on to add colour to the winter garden.

Effects with Grasses

The evergreen grass, *Stipa arundinacea*, which thrives in dry shade, can be used in a similar but altogether more stunning way, by being underplanted with a skirt of *Bergenia cordifolia*. The impact of the bergenias' purple-tinged, heart-shaped leaves beneath the arching orange-brown fronds of the grass is heightened when rose-red to dark pink, winter flowers on dark red stems come into play.

Winter Heathers

The glowing colours of winter heathers can be strikingly combined with some of the more colourful shrubs. Varieties of *Erica carnea* and *E.* x *darleyensis* can be mixed with the colourful stems of dogwoods (*Cornus*) and some varieties of willow (*Salix*). Selections of *Calluna vulgaris* with highly coloured foliage, such as 'Beoly Gold' (bright golden yellow) or

PLANTS AT THEIR BEST

EARLY WINTER
Hamamelis mollis
Iris unguicularis
Jasminum nudiflorum
Mahonia 'Charity'
Nerine bowdenii
Pernettya, berries
Prunus x *subhirtella* 'Autumnalis'
Pyracantha, berries
Sarcococca
Viburnum

MID-WINTER
Chimonanthus praecox
Eranthis hyemalis
Erica carnea
Erica x *darleyensis*
Galanthus nivalis
Garrya elliptica
Ilex, berries
Lonicera fragrantissima
Sarcococca

LATE WINTER
Crocus
Daphne mezereum
Eranthis hyemalis
Garrya elliptica
Helleborus
Iris unguicularis
Jasminum nudiflorum
Prunus x *subhirtella* 'Autumnalis'
Viburnum

'Robert Chapman' (gold turning orange-red) will also complement plants with interesting stems. Many heathers look good when matched with shrubs such as *Viburnum* x *bodnantense* 'Dawn' or white-stemmed birches such as *Betula utilis* var. *jacquemontii*.

Jobs To Do

Go outdoors whenever the weather allows – there is always tidying up to be done. When you are forced to stay indoors, take the opportunity to look at seed and plant catalogues and do any necessary planning. Later in the season you can start sowing indoors.

You can take hardwood cuttings from shrubs, and some plants can be propagated by taking root cuttings. Chrysanthemums that are overwintered in a greenhouse or cold frame are usually propagated from cuttings once the old stool (clump of roots) starts to produce shoots. You can also take dahlia cuttings.

Late winter is a good time to sow the majority of the frost-tender plants used for summer bedding, if you have a heated greenhouse. Because you need a lot of each kind of bedding, it is normally best to sow in seed trays rather than pots. Sow more sweet peas and pinch out the tips of autumn-sown ones to encourage bushier growth in the spring.

Throughout winter keep a regular eye on bulbs, corms and tubers in store as well as bulbs grown in pots for early flowering.

Above: Between now and early spring wash all your pots and canes with a garden disinfectant to prevent the spread of diseases.

Protect Hellebores

1 Protect winter hellebore flowers by placing a cloche over them. Close up each end if severe weather is expected.

2 Alternatively, lay a few bricks on either side of the plant and lay a sheet of clean glass across the top of the bricks.

Take Root Cuttings

1 Lift a young but well established plant. If it has large, fleshy roots, cut some off close to the main stem or root.

3 Insert the cuttings using a dibber or pencil to make the hole. The top of the cutting should be flush with the top of the compost.

2 Cut each root into lengths about 5cm (2in) long. To help you remember which way up they are, cut them horizontally at the top and diagonally at the bottom. Fill a pot with gritty compost (soil mix).

4 Sprinkle a thin layer of grit over the surface. Label and place in a cold frame or greenhouse. Keep the compost just moist.

5 Check the cuttings regularly until the roots are established and new shoots appear. Separate the cuttings and pot-on into individual 8cm (3in) pots.

PLANTS TO GROW FROM ROOT CUTTINGS

Acanthus
Echinops
Gaillardia
Phlox (border)
Primula denticulata

TAKE CHRYSANTHEMUM CUTTINGS

1 Take cuttings when your boxes or pots of chrysanthemum stools have produced shoots about 5cm (2in) long. Choose ones coming directly from the base of the plant. Cut them off close to the base.

3 Dip the ends in a rooting hormone to improve the rate and speed of rooting. If using a powder, dip the end in water first. Shake off any excess rooting hormone before planting.

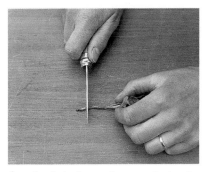

2 Pull off the lowest leaves and trim the ends of the cuttings straight across with a sharp knife.

4 Insert the cuttings around the edge of a pot containing a mixture suitable for cuttings. Then place in a propagator or cover with a plastic bag, inflated so that it does not touch the leaves. Check occasionally and remove any rotted specimens. Remove the bag completely when all the plants have rooted.

Left: Take chrysanthemum cuttings now for a supply next year.

Sow Bedding Plants

1 Fill the seed tray with a sterilized compost (soil mix) suitable for seeds and seedlings. Strike the compost off level with the rim of the tray using a piece of wood or suitable instrument.

2 Use a presser board (a scrap of wood cut to the right size will do) and press the compost gently until it is firmed about 1cm (½in) below the rim. Then water the tray.

GARDENER'S TIP

Very fine seeds, like lobelia and begonia, are difficult to handle and to spread evenly. Mix them with a small quantity of silver sand to add bulk.

---

3 Very large seeds can be spaced by hand, but most medium-sized seeds are more easily scattered with a folded piece of stiff paper. Tap it with a finger as you move it over the surface. Separate any seeds that fall together with the tip of a pencil or plant marker.

4 Unless the packet advises not to cover the seeds because they are so small, cover them by sifting more of the sowing compost over the top.

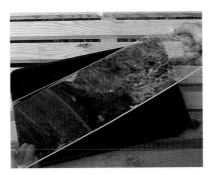

5 Unless you are placing the tray in a propagator, cover it with a sheet of glass or place it in a plastic bag. Turn the glass or bag inside-out regularly to prevent condensation drips. Remove the covering when the first seeds start to germinate.

Seasonal Plant Chart

*Plants marked with * require acid soil; those marked with ^ prefer alkaline soil.*
Planting positions: (s) sun; (ps) partial shade; (fs) full shade.

Latin name	Sow	Plant out	Season of interest and colour
Acer (s)	N/A	autumn/spring	autumn foliage
Achillea (s)	spring, in situ	N/A	summer, yellow/autumn, pink
Allium (s)	spring	autumn	summer, autumn
Alyssum (s)	spring/autumn	summer	summer, yellow or white
Anemone blanda (s, ps)	spring	autumn	spring, blue, pink, white
Aster (s, ps)	spring/autumn	autumn/spring	early autumn, violet-purple
Aubrieta (s)	autumn/spring	spring/autumn	late spring, mauve
Berberis (s, ps)	N/A	autumn/spring	autumn foliage, berries
Bergenia (s, ps)	spring	summer	spring, pink
Buddleja (s)	N/A	autumn/spring	summer, mauve, pink, white
Calluna vulgaris * (s)	N/A	autumn/spring	summer, autumn, pink, white
Canna (s)	spring/autumn	early summer	summer, autumn, red, yellow
Chimonanthus praecox (s)	spring	autumn/spring	winter, yellow
Chionodoxa (s)	late spring	autumn	early spring, blue, pink
Choisya ternata (s)	N/A	autumn/spring	late spring, autumn, white
Chrysanthemum (s)	early spring	early summer	early autumn, many colours
Clematis summer-flowering (s, ps)	N/A	autumn/spring	summer, many colours
Clematis viticella (s, ps)	N/A	autumn/spring	summer, autumn, blue, purple
Colchicum autumnale (s)	N/A	summer	autumn, pink
Cortaderia selloana (s)	spring	summer	late summer, plumes
Cotinus coggygria 'Royal Purple' (s, ps)	N/A	autumn/spring	year-round, purple foliage
Crocosmia 'Lucifer' (s, ps)	N/A	spring	summer, red

Latin name	Sow	Plant out	Season of interest and colour
Crocus (s)	N/A	autumn	late winter/early spring, many colours
Dahlia (s)	spring	summer	late summer/early autumn, many colours
Delphinium (s)	spring	autumn	summer, blue, pink, white
Dianthus (s)	spring	early summer	summer, pink, white, red
Doronicum (ps)	spring	autumn	spring, yellow
Echium vulgare 'Blue Bedder' (s)	summer	spring	summer, blue
Eranthis hyemalis (s)	spring	autumn	winter/early spring, yellow
Erica carnea * (s)	N/A	autumn	winter, purple-pink
Erica cinerea * (s)	N/A	autumn	summer, white, pink, purple
Forsythia (s)	N/A	autumn	spring, yellow
Fuchsia hybrids (s, ps)	spring	autumn	summer, pink, mauve
Galanthus nivalis (ps)	spring	autumn	winter, white
Garrya elliptica (s)	N/A	autumn/spring	winter, spring catkins
Geranium (s, ps)	spring	autumn	early summer, pink, mauve
Gladiolus (s)	spring	early summer	summer, many colours
Gloxinia (ps)	spring	autumn	summer, pink, lavender
Gypsophila ^ (s)	spring, in situ	N/A	summer, white, pink
Hamamelis mollis (s, ps)	N/A	autumn/spring	winter, yellow, orange
Hedera (s, fs)	N/A	autumn/spring	year-round foliage
Helenium (s)	spring	autumn	summer, orange, yellow
Helleborus niger (ps)	N/A	autumn/spring	winter, white

Seasonal Plant Chart

Latin name	Sow	Plant out	Season of interest and colour
Hosta (fs)	N/A	autumn/spring	year-round foliage
Hyacinthus (s)	N/A	autumn	spring, many colours
Hydrangea (s, ps)	N/A	autumn/spring	summer/early autumn, white, blue, pink
Ilex (s)	N/A	autumn/spring	winter, berries
Iris unguicularis (s)	N/A	early summer	winter, white, lavender, blue
Jasminum nudiflorum (s, ps)	N/A	autumn	winter, yellow
Juniperus (s)	N/A	autumn/spring	year-round foliage
Kniphofia (s, ps)	spring	early summer	summer, red, orange
Lathyrus odoratus (s)	spring	early summer	summer, many colours
Lavandula (s)	spring	autumn	summer, lavender
Lilium * (s, ps)	N/A	autumn	summer, many colours
Liriope muscari (fs)	spring	early summer	autumn, winter, purple
Lobelia erinus (ps)	spring	early summer	summer, many colours
Lobularia maritima (s)	spring	early summer	summer, white, pink
Lonicera fragrantissima (ps)	spring	autumn	winter, yellow, pink
Magnolia stellata * (s, ps)	N/A	autumn/spring	spring, white
Mahonia (fs)	N/A	autumn/spring	winter/spring, yellow
Miscanthus (s, ps)	early spring	autumn	year-round foliage
Muscari armeniacum (s)	spring	autumn	late winter, early spring, blue
Myosotis (s)	spring, in situ	N/A	early summer, blue
Narcissus (s)	N/A	autumn	spring, white, yellow
Nerine bowdenii (s)	N/A	spring	autumn, pink
Nicotiana (s, ps)	spring, in situ	N/A	summer, many colours
Paeonia (s, ps)	N/A	autumn/spring	early summer, many colours
Papaver orientale (s)	spring	early summer	early summer, scarlet
Papaver somniferum (s)	spring, in situ	N/A	summer, mauve, red, white
Pelargonium (s)	late winter/ early spring	summer	summer, red, pink

Latin name	Sow	Plant out	Season of interest and colour
Penstemon (s, ps)	spring	early summer	summer, many colours
Perovskia atriplicifolia (s)	N/A	autumn/spring	late summer, blue
Petunia (s)	spring	summer	summer, pink, purple
Philadelphus (s, ps)	N/A	autumn/spring	early summer, white
Primula x *polyantha* (s, ps)	early spring	autumn	spring, many colours
Primula vulgaris (ps)	early spring	autumn	spring, purple
Pulsatilla vulgaris (s)	N/A	autumn/spring	late winter, yellow
Pyracantha (s, ps)	N/A	autumn/spring	autumn berries
Ranunculus ficaria (fs)	spring	autumn	spring, yellow
Rhododendron * (ps)	N/A	autumn/spring	spring, many colours
Ribes sanguineum (s)	N/A	autumn/spring	spring, pinkish white
Romneya coulteri (s)	spring	autumn	summer, white
Rosa (s)	N/A	autumn/spring	summer, many colours
Rudbeckia (s)	spring	autumn	summer, autumn, yellow
Salvia splendens (s)	spring	summer	summer, red
Schizostylis coccinea (s)	spring	autumn	autumn, pink, red
Sedum spectabile (s)	autumn	spring	early autumn, pink
Solidago (s)	N/A	autumn/spring	late summer/early spring, white
Spiraea 'Arguta' (s)	N/A	autumn/spring	spring, white
Stachys byzantina (s)	autumn/spring	autumn/spring	summer, purple
Stipa arundinacea (s, ps)	spring	autumn	year-round foliage
Tagetes (s)	spring	summer	summer, orange, yellow
Trillium (fs)	spring	autumn	spring, white
Tropaeolum majus (s)	spring	summer	summer, orange, red
Tulipa (s)	N/A	autumn	spring, many colours
Verbena (s)	autumn, spring	summer	summer, pink, purple, white
Viburnum x *bodnantense* (s, ps)	N/A	autumn/spring	winter, pink
Viburnum tinus (s, ps)	N/A	autumn/spring	winter, white
Viola Universal (s, ps)	summer	autumn	winter, many colours
Zinnia (s)	spring	summer	summer, orange, yellow

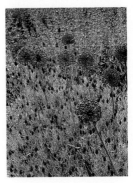

Seasonal Tasks

KNOWING WHEN TO DO JOBS IS THE SECRET OF EVERY SUCCESSFUL GARDEN. THIS QUICK GUIDE SUMMARIZES IMPORTANT GARDEN AND MAINTENANCE TASKS ACCORDING TO SEASON. THE JOBS HAVE BEEN LISTED IN THE ORDER THEY GENERALLY WOULD NEED TO BE DONE.

SPRING
The Garden
- Finish planting bare-root trees and shrubs
- Plant container-grown shrubs
- Plant herbaceous perennial plants
- Feed and mulch beds and borders
- Plant gladioli and summer bulbs
- Buy seeds and bulbs if not already done
- Sow sweet peas in pots early
- Stake perennial plants
- Sow hardy annuals
- Plant out sweet peas that have been raised in pots and sow outdoors where they are to flower
- Plant ranunculus tubers
- Harden off tender bedding plants

The Greenhouse
- Take chrysanthemum cuttings
- Start begonia and gloxinia tubers into growth
- Pot up pelargoniums and fuchsia cuttings rooted earlier
- Pot up chrysanthemums rooted earlier. Pot these on later in the season
- Take dahlia cuttings. Pot these on later in the season if they need it
- Sow seeds of bedding and pot plants
- Prick out or pot up seedlings sown earlier

SUMMER
The Garden
- Dead-head border plants regularly
- Stake perennial plants
- Sow hardy annuals and biennials
- Plant dahlias, gladioli and summer bulbs
- Prune lilac, philadelphus, spiraea and broom after flowering
- Finish hardening off and planting tender bedding plants
- Pinch out growing tip from early flowering chrysanthemums
- Watch out for signs of mildew and aphids on roses. Spray promptly
- Hoe beds and borders regularly to keep down weeds
- Divide and replant border irises
- Take semi-ripe cuttings
- Layer shrubs and carnations
- Plant colchicums, to flower in autumn
- Transplant biennials and perennial seedlings to a nursery bed
- Feed plants in containers to keep blooms coming
- Start planting spring-flowering bulbs
- Take fuchsia and pelargonium cuttings
- Prune rambler roses

- Feed and disbud dahlias and chrysanthemums as necessary
- Transplant polyanthus seedlings into their flowering positions

The Greenhouse
- Take leaf and semi-ripe cuttings
- Keep a watch for pests and diseases. Spray promptly or try a biological control
- Sow spring-flowering plants such as cyclamen, schizanthus and exacums
- Take leaf and semi-ripe cuttings

AUTUMN
The Garden
- Plant spring-flowering bulbs
- Take fuchsia and pelargonium cuttings
- Plant lilies
- Clear summer bedding and prepare for spring bedding plants
- Disbud dahlias and chrysanthemums as necessary
- Lift and store dahlias after the first frost
- Lift and store gladioli and other tender bulbs, corms and tubers

- Plant roses
- Plant bare-root and balled trees and shrubs
- Plant perennial plants
- Take in tender fuchsias and pelargoniums
- Protect vulnerable plants that will remain in the garden
- Lift and take in chrysanthemums not hardy enough to overwinter outside
- Plant lilies
- Sow sweet peas in pots
- Cut down the dead tops of herbaceous perennials
- Take hardwood shrub cuttings
- Protect crowns of vulnerable perennials such as delphiniums and lupins from slugs

The Greenhouse
- Sow spring-flowering plants such as cyclamen, schizanthus and exacums
- Pot up and pot on seedling pot plants as it becomes necessary

WINTER
The Garden
- Plant bare-root and balled trees and shrubs
- Check bulbs being grown in pots for early flowering
- Protect vulnerable plants that will remain in the garden
- Take hardwood shrub cuttings
- Take root cuttings

- Protect flowers of winter plants that might be spoilt by the weather
- Knock heavy snow off hedges and conifers if branches start to bend under the weight
- Insulate the cold frame against the coldest weather
- Plant climbers
- Feed and mulch beds and borders
- Sow sweet peas in pots
- Pinch out growing tips of autumn-sown sweet peas

The Greenhouse
- Once a week check all plants and pick off any dead or dying leaves before they start to rot
- Start off overwintered chrysanthemum stools (roots) to provide cuttings
- Take chrysanthemum cuttings
- Pot up chrysanthemums rooted earlier
- Take dahlia cuttings
- Sow seeds of bedding plants and pot plants
- Prick out seedlings sown earlier
- Increase ventilation on warm days

Common Names of Plants

aconite *Aconitum*
African marigold *Tagetes erecta*
Algerian iris *Iris unguicularis*
Autumn crocus *Colchicum autumnale*
bleeding heart *Dicentra spectabilis*
borage *Borago officicinalis*
broom *Genista*
busy Lizzie *Impatiens*
buttercup *Ranunculus*
candytuft *Iberis*
canterbury bells *Campanula medium*
coneflower *Rudbeckia*
cupid's dart *Catanache*
daisy *Bellis perennis*
daylily *Hemerocallis*
dogwood *Cornus*
dog's tooth violet *Erythronium*
elephant's ears *Bergenia*
evening primrose *Oenothera speciosa*
forget-me-not *Mysotis*
French marigold *Tagetes patula*
globeflower *Trollius*
grape hyacinth *Muscari*
hazel *Corylus*
hellebore *Helleborus*
holly *Ilex*
hollyhock *Alcea rosea*
ironweed *Vernonia*
Japanese anemone *Anemone* x *blanda*
japonica *Chaenomeles*
Jerusalem cross *Lychnis chalcedonica*
kaffir lily *Schizolstylis coccinea*
kingcup *Caltha*
lady's mantle *Alchemilla mollis*
larkspur *Consolida ambigua*
leopard's bane *Doronicum*
lilac *Syringa*

lilyturf *Liriope*
love-in-a-mist *Nigella*
lungwort *Pulmonaria*
Madonna lily *Lilium candidum*
Michaelmas daisy *Aster*
montbretia *Crocosmia*
nasturtium *Tropaeolum majus*
pampas grass *Cortaderia selloana*
poppy, field *Papaver rhoeas*
poppy, opium *Papaver somniferum*
pot marigold *Calendula*
primrose *Primula vulgaris*
red hot poker *Kniphofia*
Siberian wallflower *Erysimum* x *allioni*
snapdragon *Antirrhinum*
snowdrop *Galanthus*
snowflake *Leucojum*
stock *Matthiola*
stonecrop *Sedum*
sunflower *Helianthus*
sweet pea *Lathyrus odoratus*
sweet violet *Viola odorata*
tobacco plant *Nicotiana alata*
wallflower *Erysimum*
willow *Salix*
winter aconite *Eranthis hyemalis*
winter-flowering pansies *Viola* x
      wittrockiana Universal Series
winter jasmine *Jasminum nudiflorum*
witch hazel *Hamamelis*
wood anemone *Anemone nemerosa*
wood lily *Trillium*
yarrow *Achillea*
yew *Taxus*

Index

Index